The Presidency

PROJECT SECOND CHANCE
CONTRA COSTA COUNTY LIBRARY

E PLURIBUS UNUM

The Presidency

Brendan January

CONTRA COSTA COUNTY LIBRARY

Franklin Watts
A Division of Scholastic Inc.
New York • Toronto • London • Auckland • Sydney
Mexico City • New Delhi • Hong Kong
Danbury, Connecticut

3 1901 03698 4757

Note to readers: Definitions for words in **bold** can be found in the Glossary at the back of this book.

The illustration on the cover shows the White House. The photograph opposite the title page shows the Oval Office.

Photographs © 2004: AP/Wide World Photos: 5 left, 44 top, 44 bottom; Bridgeman Art Library International Ltd., London/New York/New-York Historical Society, New York, USA: 6, 7; Corbis Images: 5 right, 12 top, 17, 19, 26, 36, 41, 42, 46 (Bettmann), 10 (Joseph Sohm/ChromoSohm Inc.), 32 (Oscar White), 22, 28, 29, 45; Folio, Inc./John Skowronski: cover; Franklin D. Roosevelt Presidential Library and Museum: 20, 21; Getty Images: 31 (David Hume Kennerly), 12 bottom (Shauna McRoberts/US Army), 48 (Pictorial Parade); Library of Congress: 35 (via SODA), 14, 38; NASA: 50; North Wind Picture Archives: 24; White House Historical Association/Bruce White: 2.

Library of Congress Cataloging-in-Publication Data

January, Brendan.
The Presidency / Brendan January.
p. cm. — (Watts library)
Published simultaneously in Canada.
Includes bibliographical references and index.
ISBN 0-531-12293-X (lib. bdg.) 0-531-16383-0 (pbk.)
1. Presidents—United States—Juvenile literature. 2. Presidents—United States—History—Juvenile literature. I. Title. II. Series.
JK517.J36 2004
973'.09'9—dc22

2004002007

© 2004 by Scholastic Inc.
All rights reserved. Published simultaneously in Canada.
Printed in the United States of America.
1 2 3 4 5 6 7 8 9 10 R 13 12 11 10 09 08 07 06 05 04

Contents

Chapter One
Something New 7

Chapter Two
Leader of the Nation 15

Chapter Three
Commander in Chief 23

Chapter Four
Life, Work, and Play 33

Chapter Five
Assassination and Scandal 39

Chapter Six
Into the Future 47

52 **Timeline**

55 **Glossary**

57 **To Find Out More**

60 **A Note on Sources**

61 **Index**

George Washington was sworn in as president of the United States on April 30, 1789.

Chapter One

Something New

On the morning of April 30, 1789, a carriage carried George Washington over the cobblestoned and muddy streets of New York City. Washington was dressed for an important occasion. He wore an elegant brown suit with white silk stockings. A dress sword hung from his belt.

Along the way, crowds of citizens gathered. Washington was the young nation's hero. Years before, he had led the ragtag American army to victory over the British in the Revolutionary War.

When the war ended in 1783, Washington eagerly took off his uniform. He told friends that he hoped to retire to Mount Vernon, his beloved Virginia plantation. The country, however, had called Washington to service again.

The carriage stopped at Wall Street in front of Federal Hall, an elegant brick building with white columns. The coach door swung open. Washington walked into the structure, climbed a flight of stairs, and appeared with a group of men on a balcony overlooking the street. Below, thousands of people watched silently. A special ceremony began.

Washington solemnly placed his hand on a bible held out by Robert Livingston, Chancellor of the state of New York. Livingston said an oath, which Washington repeated. After he finished, Washington leaned over and kissed the bible.

Livingston turned to the people waiting below. "It is done!" he shouted. "Long live George Washington, President of the United States!" The crowd exploded in cheers. Church

The Oath of the President of the United States

"I, do solemnly swear [or affirm] that I will faithfully execute the Office of President of the United States, and will to the best of my ability, preserve, protect and defend the Constitution of the United States."

The First President

No person shaped the office of the president as much as George Washington during his two terms. There had never been a president before. Washington's every word and action would become a model for other presidents.

It was a tremendous responsibility, and Washington knew it. He understood that his every move would become a **precedent**. "As the first of every thing in our situation will serve to establish a Precedent," Washington wrote to a friend, "it is devoutly wished on my part, that these precedents may be fixed on true principles."

bells rang through the city in celebration. The United States had sworn in its first president.

When Washington was inaugurated, he was the only president in the world. Kings, princes, and wealthy families ruled Europe. An emperor sat upon the throne in China. A czar controlled Russia. No one had ever heard of a ruler called a "president."

The Making of the Presidency

The presidency was created in the summer of 1787. Worried that the current **federal government** was too weak, fifty-five powerful Americans gathered in Philadelphia to discuss a new government. This meeting has been called the **Constitutional Convention**. They met in the city's majestic brick statehouse and closed the windows so passersby couldn't hear. Through the hot summer months they debated and wrote. By autumn, they were finished. The result was an extraordinary document called the Constitution.

The Constitution is a plan, or a blueprint, for the United States government. Nothing quite like it had ever been attempted before. Using ideas first suggested in Europe, the statesmen created a government with three branches. The legislative branch is **Congress**. The judicial branch is made up of judges and the federal courts. The executive branch is the presidency.

Why are there three branches? Each has a role in governing the nation, and the Constitution was written to keep any

Done in Convention by the Unanimous Consent of the States present the Seventeen
Day of September in the Year of our Lord one thousand seven hundred and Eighty seven
of the Independance of the United States of America the Twelfth In Witness
We have hereunto subscribed our Names,

The Constitution was signed by thirty-nine of the fifty-five delegates to the Constitutional Convention.

Naming a Leader

The Constitutional Convention spent a long time debating titles for the executive, including "His Elective Majesty," "His Elective Highness," and "His Mightiness." They settled on "Mr. President."

one branch from growing too strong. The Americans remembered bitterly how British rulers had disregarded the rights of American colonists. To prevent this from happening again, the Constitution gave each branch rights over the other branches, creating a system called **checks and balances**.

The Constitution gives the presidency many powers. The president has the right to **veto**, or reject, laws and legislation passed by Congress. The president appoints the judges who sit on the Supreme Court and can **pardon**, or excuse, citizens of their crimes. The president is the head of the armed forces and is responsible for negotiating relations with other nations.

An Office and a Person

The office of the presidency is far more than the powers listed in the Constitution. The president has many different roles. The president is the nation's highest and most visible leader. With a single speech, the president can determine how the country will spend its resources and what problems deserve attention. By appearing at the scene of a disaster, the president can bring order and calm.

The president must also make difficult decisions about war

SANCHEZ
U.S. ARMY
OLD IRONSIDES

and peace. As the leader of the armed forces, the president must often decide whether to send American soldiers into combat. Presidents have also used their office to urge warring nations to settle their differences peacefully.

The presidency is also a person. Each president confronted different problems, and each president used the office differently to solve them. "No president wants to fail," said President Lyndon B. Johnson. "You do the best you know how."

This book examines the two sides of the presidency—the office and the person. Since George Washington took the first presidential oath in New York City in 1789, there have been forty-three presidents of the United States. The nation has grown from a country of 4 million people to a nation of more than 290 million people. The presidency has become the most powerful leadership position in the world.

Presidents have played a leading role in military conflicts. President Franklin D. Roosevelt guided the nation through World War II. Most recently, President George W. Bush has overseen U.S. military action in Iraq.

To win the election, President Andrew Jackson relied on support from average citizens.

Chapter Two

Leader of the Nation

Today, the president can exercise enormous power. The president can propose laws that will change the way people live, order thousands of soldiers to any spot on Earth, and convince other leaders to solve their problems in peace. But the president can do little unless he or she is supported by the American people.

Many U.S. presidents have developed a close bond with everyday citizens. After Andrew Jackson's inauguration in April 1829, his enthusiastic supporters decided to celebrate in the White House. They followed Jackson into the East Room, where they shattered crystal and china while helping themselves to trays of drinks. The carpet was left smeared with mud, upholstery was torn, and curtains were ripped.

Some observers were disgusted. "The country is ruined," wrote Congressman John Randolph.

Jackson, however, used this support to increase the power of the presidency. Few presidents before had vetoed laws coming out of Congress. But Jackson began striking down laws at a speed that shocked observers. Critics began calling him "King Andrew."

Jackson was also firm when South Carolina lawmakers threatened to disobey federal laws. "Disunion by armed force is treason," he said, and he prepared an army to march on South Carolina. Resistance collapsed.

Two for the Price of One

The presidency is often dominated by two people—the president and the president's spouse. First ladies, such as Eleanor Roosevelt, used the presidency to promote issues of public health and world peace. Hillary Rodham Clinton developed a plan for national health care.

When presidents were ill or injured, it was often the first lady who controlled the White House and determined who got to see the president. Nancy Reagan protected Ronald Reagan while he was recovering from gunshot wounds. Edith Wilson nursed her husband, Woodrow Wilson, after he suffered a stroke. When Grover Cleveland had surgery for cancer of the mouth, his wife Frances made sure only a few people learned about it.

Jackson remained one of the nation's most popular presidents. Even after his death, citizens continued to vote for Jackson in presidential elections by writing his name on the ballot.

Hooverville

Not all presidents were as popular as Andrew Jackson. One president who failed to reassure Americans was Herbert Hoover. When Hoover was elected president in 1928, the United States was enjoying an economic boom. Jobs were plentiful. The roads were choked with newly purchased automobiles. Wages were rising. The U.S. stock market was soaring.

Hoover was enthusiastic, claiming that the good times would keep coming. Poverty itself, Hoover said, was being

While in office, President Herbert Hoover hoped to end the nation's economic troubles. Here he is shown signing a bill to help farmers.

threatened with extinction. "The poor-house is vanishing from among us," he declared.

The good times did not last. On October 24, 1929, a day remembered as "Black Thursday," stock market prices suddenly dropped. The next Tuesday, the prices crashed as panicked investors desperately sold their stock. Most were devastated.

The President's Advisers

Though there was no provision for it in the Constitution, George Washington assembled a group of advisers known as the cabinet. The cabinet members were responsible for executive government in many areas, including banks, labor, farming, and relations with other countries. To this day, each president appoints a cabinet to run the many offices of the U.S. government.

At first, Hoover appeared unconcerned. The economy, he noted in his speeches, was still strong. Most Americans had jobs. Factories still filled orders.

The stock market crash, however, had a disastrous effect. People grew worried and stopped going to stores. Building plans were scrapped, and orders for goods slowed. Without goods to sell, factories began firing workers. Without jobs, people stopped buying goods.

The country had never seen such a **depression**. Millions of people were out of work. In cities around the country, people lined up for a tin of soup and a piece of bread. Thousands lived in misery in small villages of shacks made from scrap lumber.

These squalid settlements were nicknamed "Hoovervilles." To stop a biting winter wind, people wrapped themselves in newspaper, which was called a "Hoover blanket." When someone turned his or her pocket inside out for change that wasn't there, it was called a "Hoover flag."

In the White House, Hoover tried to cope with the crisis. He approved millions of dollars in projects, and he tried to pump money into the economy through loans. But it was not

Because of the country's poor economic situation, many people were without jobs. Some of the unemployed ended up living in small shacks.

enough. From 1929 to 1932, the number of unemployed jumped from more than one million to thirteen million people.

In the 1932 presidential election, Hoover was defeated by a New Yorker named Franklin Delano Roosevelt. Hoover kept insisting that good times were "just around the corner." Roosevelt, however, promised the nation a "New Deal."

A New Deal

The presidency would never be the same. Roosevelt suffered from a crushing disease called polio, which left his legs

President Roosevelt wanted to help the nation recover from the hard times of the Great Depression.

paralyzed and forced him to use a wheelchair. Rather than weaken Roosevelt, however, the experience made him tougher. He would not settle for failure. "If you had spent two years in bed trying to wriggle your big toe," he once remarked, "after that anything else seems easy."

On a bright, chilly March 4, 1933, Roosevelt told Americans during his inauguration speech, "the only thing we have to fear is fear itself." He promised "action, and action now."

In the first hundred days of Roosevelt's first **term** of office, the federal government enacted dozens of plans to shore up the banking system and get the economy moving again. The government also pursued ways to provide work for the unemployed. The Tennessee Valley Authority Act funded the construction of dams. The Public Works Administration began hundreds of construction projects. Young men who were employed by the Civilian Conservation Corps received food and wages. In 1935, Roosevelt's Social Security Act was passed. The act taxed workers' pay and distributed the money to the elderly, the unemployed, the needy, and the blind.

Roosevelt began using the radio to communicate directly to the American people. His first "fireside chat" drew 60

Two Terms Is Enough

After Franklin D. Roosevelt won four terms as president, lawmakers decided it was necessary to prevent one person from ever holding so much power again. The Twenty-Second Amendment to the Constitution, which limits the president to two terms, was proposed in 1947 and ratified, or approved, in 1951.

million listeners. Through Roosevelt's reforms, his "fireside chats," his projects and aid, the government became a greater part of people's lives than it ever had before. This angered many, who insisted that the government needed to stay small. Roosevelt's popularity, however, only grew. In 1940, Roosevelt did something no other president had done. He ran for a third term and won. He won again in 1944.

By the time Roosevelt died in 1945, he had changed the role of government in American life and the role of the president in history. After Roosevelt, Americans looked to the government to solve problems in the economy. They also looked to the government for help and aid.

To get Americans working again, Roosevelt established many programs, such as the Civilian Conservation Corps (CCC). Enrollees in CCC, shown here, work on a highway project.

The president is the country's military leader, responsible for U.S. troops around the world.

Chapter Three

Commander in Chief

In the last fifty years, the president of United States has controlled the largest and strongest military force in history. With one command, the president can launch nuclear missiles or send American forces to anywhere on Earth.

The decision to use military force, as Bill Clinton once said, is never an easy one. By his or her actions in wartime, a president can become one of the greatest leaders in history or can be driven from office.

The outbreak of violence over the whiskey tax is known as the Whiskey Tax Rebellion. It was one of the first times a president had to use military force to settle a conflict within the country.

Rebellions and Civil War

The first time a sitting president led an army was in 1794. In that year, the government decided to tax a liquor called whiskey. Farmers in western Pennsylvania were outraged. A tax collector was tarred and feathered by an angry mob. The rest gathered guns and marched on Pittsburgh. President George Washington saw the rebellion as a threat to the government's authority. He assembled an army of 12,000 men and marched into Pennsylvania. The rebellion quickly collapsed.

When Abraham Lincoln was elected president in 1860, the United States broke apart. Some southern states, fearing that Lincoln would try to end slavery, **seceded** to form their own nation called the Confederate States of America.

In response to the crisis, Lincoln used the powers of the

presidency in a way no president had before. Declaring the secession an "emergency," he called upon states to furnish soldiers that would crush the rebellion. He declared that the United States Navy would surround the southern states in a **blockade**. No southern ships would be permitted to enter or leave. To fight southern sympathizers and spies, Lincoln suspended the writ of Habeas Corpus, which protected important individual legal rights. He did all this without asking Congress or the Supreme Court.

"The World Must Be Made Safe for Democracy"

In April 1917, President Woodrow Wilson joined the French and the English in a war against Germany. The United States would fight because, he said, "the world must be made safe for democracy."

When the war ended with victory in 1918, Wilson hoped for a fair peace. France, Great Britain, and Italy, however, had suffered millions of dead and wounded. They were determined to make Germany pay. Their leaders thought Wilson was naïve and his suggestions unrealistic. Wilson especially pushed for a new organization called the League of Nations, where countries could discuss and work out their problems with words rather than with guns and bullets.

The League of Nations was written into the final treaty, but Wilson faced resistance from Congress. Many senators wanted the United States to turn inward and not bother with

Woodrow Wilson traveled the country, hoping to convince people that the United States should join the League of Nations.

the problems of the world. Realizing that Congress would vote down the league, Wilson decided to take his cause directly to the American people. Wilson rode through the West and Midwest in a train car, making thirty-seven speeches in twenty-two days. The trip exhausted Wilson. On October 2, 1919, he suffered a stroke that left him partially paralyzed.

Wilson was too weak to join the debates about the league. After he unwisely rejected a compromise from Congress, the bill went down to defeat. The League of Nations was created but without the United States as a member. Wilson never recovered. He died in 1924.

Truman Fires a General

Presidents in wartime have to ensure that they, not the generals, maintain control of the military. This is sometimes difficult. In 1951, North Korean troops stormed into South Korea. The North Koreans were communists supported by the Soviet Union. At that time, the United States was in a worldwide struggle to prevent the spread of communism. That struggle had come to Korea.

With the permission of the United Nations, President Harry S. Truman ordered U.S. troops to fight alongside the South Koreans. General Douglas MacArthur, a war hero from World War II, took command. He ordered a brilliant counterattack, and soon the North Korean army was retreating in disarray.

There was, however, a growing problem. As the Americans advanced north, they approached the North Korean border with China. China was an enormous Communist nation.

Truman did not want a war with China, and he strongly warned MacArthur to keep away from the Chinese border. But MacArthur ignored Truman. When American units continued north, the Chinese leaders secretly directed soldiers to help North Korea beat back MacArthur's army. The Soviet Union also sent fighters into combat, disguised in North Korean uniforms. As the Americans retreated, MacArthur urged a counterattack against China itself. Truman, fearing a new world war against China and the Soviet Union, said no.

MacArthur angrily challenged Truman's policy. Worse, MacArthur offered to discuss ending the war with North Korean leaders, a task normally handled only by the president. Truman had seen enough. He fired the popular MacArthur.

The State of the Union

Every year, the president gives a State of the Union message to Congress. The president can use the speech to address problems or issues facing the nation. The president can also introduce new ideas and programs for the coming year.

The president has authority over all of the branches of the military. When President Truman discovered that U.S. Army General Douglas MacArthur had disobeyed his orders, he fired MacArthur.

The decision angered many in the United States. Truman, however, had simply used the powers of the presidency. He reminded MacArthur and all generals that the president, a **civilian**, is in control of the armed forces. Not the other way around.

"I didn't fire him because he was . . . dumb . . . although he was," Truman said. He fired MacArthur because he wouldn't respect the authority of the president.

Johnson and the Vietnam War

President Johnson announces that the United States will retaliate against North Vietnam for attacking U.S. ships.

Sometimes, the country decides that the president should not wage war. In August 1964, President Lyndon B. Johnson made a startling announcement. Two American destroyers cruising in the Gulf of Tonkin off the coast of North Vietnam had been fired upon by North Vietnamese torpedo boats, he said.

On August 5, Johnson went to Congress and asked for special powers to give the president the right to order military attacks against North Vietnam. Congress agreed and passed the "Tonkin Gulf Resolution." Under the resolution, Johnson was allowed to send hundreds of thousands of U.S. troops to South Vietnam, a U.S. ally.

Soon, U.S. soldiers were engaged in bitter battles against North Vietnamese soldiers and guerrilla forces. As U.S.

The War Powers Act

With the War Powers Act, Congress hoped to gain more control over how the president directs the military. This, however, has not worked well. The courts have ruled that the War Powers Act is unconstitutional. That means it violates the laws written in the Constitution. The president, not Congress, is commander in chief of the military.

soldiers died in battle, Americans at home began wondering why. As time went on, more American soldiers died, and protesters began showing up outside the White House, chanting against Johnson and protesting the war in Vietnam.

The protests became too much, and Johnson did not seek reelection in 1968. Members of Congress were determined to restrict future presidents. In 1973, they passed the War Powers Act, which requires a president to consult with Congress before starting a war.

President as Peacemaker

Other presidents have labored for peace. In 1905, Theodore Roosevelt helped Japan and Russia bring their war to an end. His efforts earned him a Nobel Peace Prize.

Jimmy Carter was determined to bring peace to the Middle East, one of the most war-torn regions of the world. Since the 1940s, Egypt and Israel had fought three wars. In 1978, Carter invited the president of Egypt, Anwar Sadat, and the prime minister of Israel, Menachem Begin, to the presidential retreat at Camp David, Maryland.

Within the peaceful camp, the two sides began tough negotiations that lasted thirteen days. When the talks stalled, Carter coaxed the two leaders into a compromise. In the end, Israel and Egypt had concluded a historic peace treaty. In March 1979, Carter traveled to the Middle East himself to ensure that the treaty didn't collapse before it was enacted. It didn't, and Carter was hailed as a peacemaker.

President Jimmy Carter helped Israeli Prime Minister Menachem Begin and Egyptian President Anwar Sadat form a peace agreement between their two countries.

Despite his failure to win reelection in 1980, Carter continued his efforts for peace. In 1994, he persuaded dictators in Haiti to step down rather than cause war. He has visited many of the world's troubled areas, including Cuba, North Korea, and war-torn Bosnia. In some cases, he has been heavily criticized for engaging dictators. Still, he insists, there is no harm in reaching out. In 2002, Carter was awarded the Nobel Peace Prize.

President Theodore Roosevelt had a very active family life. He spent a lot of time with his children and grandchildren. Here he holds a grandchild.

Chapter Four

Life, Work, and Play

Almost all of the presidents have lived in the White House. Sitting in the heart of Washington, D.C., the White House is an elegant structure where the president meets with leaders from around the world and important figures from the United States. It is also the place where the president and his family live.

President Theodore Roosevelt's large, rambunctious family filled the White House with laughter, much of it caused by Roosevelt himself. He battled his children in pillow fights. He was up at 6:00 A.M. to do push ups. The White House lawn was judged suitable for football games. Unable to enjoy just a stroll, Roosevelt went on "obstacle walks." Members of Congress and visitors, more used to generous meals and an evening in a soft chair, panted and sweated to keep up.

Roosevelt also learned that life in the White House is like life in a fish bowl. It is hard to protect your privacy when journalists, politicians, and citizens are watching your every move.

Roosevelt came under scrutiny when it was discovered that his oldest daughter, Alice, bet on horses. Roosevelt refused to do anything about it. "I can do one of two things," he said. "I can be president of the United States, or I can control Alice. I cannot possibly do both."

Do You Want this Job?

To become president, a person must be at least thirty-five years old, a natural born citizen, and a U.S. resident for fourteen years prior to election. The president is paid about $400,000 a year, as well as $50,000 for expenses and another $100,000 for travel expenses.

At Work

Each president has a different work schedule. Calvin Coolidge awoke each morning at between 7 A.M. and 9 A.M. At 12:30 P.M., he greeted social callers at the White House, who numbered several hundred a day. He then took a two-hour nap and returned to work, not stopping until evening. Not everyone was impressed. "Coolidge's chief feat," snorted a newspaper editor, "was to sleep more than any other president."

Coolidge was born and raised in Vermont, where work was emphasized and talking was not. He brought this attitude to the White House. Each visitor, it seemed, wanted a special favor or had an idea. "[Most people I meet] want something

President Calvin Coolidge was known for being a quiet person.

they ought not to have," Coolidge recalled. "If you keep dead still, they will run down in three or four minutes. If you even cough or smile, they will start up again."

Coolidge's ability to keep his mouth closed became famous, earning him the nickname "Silent Cal." But he also had a sharp sense of humor. During a dinner party, a woman came up to him and said she had bet a girlfriend that she could get him to say more than three words. "You lose," he replied.

Coolidge, however, believed it was important to talk to the people of the United States. He was the first president to hold regular meetings with members of the press, which occurred twice a week. By the end of his term, he had held 520 press conferences.

Taking a Break

Being president is one of the toughest jobs in the world. It's no wonder that each president has found a way to relax.

President Kennedy enjoyed playing with his children Caroline and John.

Thomas Jefferson went horseback riding every day. At the end of one ride, he greeted a foreign diplomat while still dressed in mud-splattered boots. Ulysses S. Grant relaxed by

speeding through the streets of Washington in a two-seat carriage. Once, a police officer stopped Grant and gave him a ticket.

When William Howard Taft ran for president, he escaped the pressure by taking up golf. He enjoyed the sport, he said, "[because] you cannot permit yourself to think of anything else."

Herbert Hoover began each day with thirty minutes of throwing around a ball on the South Lawn of the White House. Members of the staff, the cabinet, Congress, and even the press were invited to play.

John F. Kennedy enjoyed swimming in the White House pool. George H. W. Bush took breaks by pitching horseshoes. He organized the White House butlers and gardeners into leagues and never missed a tournament.

Despite his father's warnings, John Quincy Adams became the sixth president of the United States and the first son of a former president to become president.

Chapter Five

Assassination and Scandal

Why would anyone want to have a job that requires so much energy and holds so much responsibility? Many have asked that question, especially the presidents themselves.

Washington said becoming president made him feel like a criminal "who is going to his place of execution." Jefferson called it a "splendid misery" that led to a "daily loss of friends." John Adams once said, "No man who ever held the office would congratulate a friend in obtaining it." Grover Cleveland found presidential duties exhausting. "My God, what is there about this office that any man should ever want to get into it?" he once exclaimed.

Harry S. Truman recalled his emotions when he became president. "I felt like the moon, the stars, and all the planets had fallen on me," he remembered. "Boys," he said, when he met journalists for the first time, "if you ever pray, pray for me now."

Lyndon B. Johnson experienced the same emotions when he took the presidential oath on November 22, 1963, the date President John F. Kennedy was killed. Later, Johnson stood before Congress and said, "All I have I would have given gladly not to be standing here today."

Assassinations

The enormous power each president wields can make them a target. Some people think they can change history by killing a president. The first attempt on a president's life took place on January 30, 1835. A house painter named Richard Lawrence stepped in front of President Andrew Jackson as he was leaving the Capitol. Lawrence pointed two pistols directly at Jackson and pulled the triggers. Both, however, failed to fire. Lawrence was captured, declared insane, and locked up in an **asylum**.

An actor named John Wilkes Booth supported the South during the Civil War. In 1865, the South had collapsed, and the Confederate army surrendered in early April. Furious,

Being president can make the person a target for attack by people who object to the president's actions or decisions. President Abraham Lincoln was assassinated by John Wilkes Booth who was angry about the Civil War.

Booth vowed to murder Lincoln. On April 14, 1865, Lincoln hoped to relax one night at Ford's Theater in Washington, D.C. During the performance, Booth stepped quietly into the president's box and fired a single bullet into the back of Lincoln's head. Lincoln was carried into a cramped apartment across the street. Lincoln never recovered consciousness. He died on the following morning.

James Garfield survived only a few months in the presidency. An unstable man, Charles Guiteau, was angered when Garfield did not award him a government job. On July 2, 1881, Guiteau shot Garfield in a Washington, D.C., train station. Doctors were unable to locate the bullet, and Garfield died later that year on September 19.

William McKinley was shot twice in the abdomen at the Pan-American Exposition in Buffalo, New York, on September 6, 1901, and died eight days later. The assassin, Leon Czolgosz, concealed his pistol in a bandage around his hand. Czolgosz, who was unemployed and poor, hated wealthier people. He was executed in the electric chair.

On November 22, 1963, President John F. Kennedy and his wife Jackie were riding through Dallas, Texas, in the back of a limousine. The day was sunny and warm, and the limousine's protective cover had been removed. Kennedy waved to the smiling viewers that lined the route. At about 12:30 P.M., Kennedy's car passed beneath the Texas School Book Depository building. Allegedly, a man named Lee Harvey Oswald crouched by an open window on the sixth floor with a rifle. He fired several times, striking Kennedy in the neck and head. Kennedy was rushed to a hospital, but the damage was too severe. Kennedy was declared dead at 1:00 P.M.

This photograph was taken shortly before President Kennedy was shot by an assassin.

On March 30, 1981, Ronald Reagan was exiting a building in Washington, D.C., when scattered shots caused the secret service to push him into a waiting limousine. The limousine sped away to a hospital as Reagan sat in the back, bleeding from a bullet that had lodged within an inch of his heart.

Reagan was in serious danger, but he kept his sense of humor. When he saw the hospital doctors, he had one concern. "Please tell me you're Republicans," said the Republican president. Reagan would recover from his wounds.

Resigning From Office

On June 17, 1972, burglars were discovered at the headquarters for the Democratic National Committee, which was located in the Watergate office complex in Washington, D.C. At first the crime seemed minor. But then investigators discovered that advisors to President Richard Nixon, a Republican, knew about the crime. People began wondering if Nixon was involved. One of Nixon's highest aides, John Dean, told Congress that Nixon was aware of the break in and had prevented Federal Bureau of Investigation (FBI) agents from investigating it.

Another aide revealed that Nixon had used a taping system to record all his conversations in the White House. Congress wanted to hear the tapes, but Nixon refused to surrender them to Congress. The tapes, he insisted, were protected under his rights as president. In July 1974, however, the Supreme Court ruled that Nixon had to hand them over.

After a Supreme Court ruling against him, President Nixon announced that he would release tapes of his conversations.

This is the resignation letter written by President Nixon.

THE WHITE HOUSE
WASHINGTON

August 9, 1974

Dear Mr. Secretary:

I hereby resign the Office of President of the United States.

Sincerely,

Richard Nixon

11.35 AM

The Honorable Henry A. Kissinger
The Secretary of State
Washington, D.C. 20520

HK

On a recording made on June 23, 1972, Nixon told the FBI not to continue the Watergate investigation. Following the release of the tapes, support for Nixon rapidly collapsed. Facing impeachment, Nixon did something no other president has done. He resigned. On August 9, 1974, Nixon stepped out onto the White House lawn for the last time and into a waiting helicopter.

"My fellow Americans," said the new president, Gerald R. Ford, "our long national nightmare is over."

Ford then made a fateful decision. He used the power of the president to pardon Nixon. Nixon never had to face a formal investigation or punishment for "Watergate." Although some people were angered by Ford's decision, many critics have come to see his decision as responsible and wise. "It was an extraordinary act of courage," said Senator Edward Kennedy in 2001.

Still, Nixon's resignation was a devastating blow to the presidency. Many Americans felt angry, disappointed, and even disgusted with many of their political leaders. "Watergate" became a symbol of everything that was wrong with the U.S. government.

Facing Impeachment

Andrew Johnson became president after Lincoln was murdered in 1865. Johnson and Congress soon argued over Reconstruction, or the process of bringing the southern states back into the Union after the Civil War. When Johnson refused to go along with Congress's plan, a group in Congress decided to impeach him. One vote in the Senate prevented Johnson's removal. Congress, however, had made its point. It controlled Reconstruction for the next several years.

In took more than one hundred years for the next president to be impeached. In the 1990s, President Bill Clinton lied under oath about a relationship he had had with a young intern named Monica Lewinsky. When the lie was discovered, members in the House of Representatives voted to impeach the president. A trial was held in the Senate, but the senators did not vote to remove Clinton from office.

A Thanksgiving Pardon

Every year, the president pardons a turkey just before Thanksgiving. Instead of ending up on a dinner table, the bird is taken to a petting zoo to live out its life in peace.

President Johnson faced an impeachment trial in the Senate for not agreeing with Congress's plans for rebuilding the South after the Civil War.

One of Thomas Jefferson's greatest contributions as president was expanding the size of the country and calling for exploration of the West.

Chapter Six

Into the Future

The president has led the nation not only in war and peace, but also into the unknown. In the early 1800s, the United States occupied only the eastern area of North America. The vast western lands, their peoples and animal life, were mostly unknown to Americans. Thomas Jefferson was determined to change this.

Jefferson organized an expedition to chart a route west and explore the region. Jefferson gave command to his private secretary, Meriwether Lewis. Lewis asked an army officer, William Clark, to help.

In spring 1804, Lewis and Clark left St. Louis. They packed more than forty

The President and TV

In 1960, a funny thing happened after two presidential candidates, John F. Kennedy and Richard Nixon, debated each other. One half of the nation thought Kennedy had won the debate. the other half believed it was Nixon who won. The difference? Television. On TV, Kennedy appeared trim, calm, and well dressed. Nixon appeared agitated and unsure. To radio listeners, however, Nixon's arguments were more convincing. To them, Nixon was the winner. Since then, presidents have recognized the importance of TV. They pick clothing to show strength or warmth. For example, when Jimmy Carter wanted to appear friendly, he wore a sweater. Presidents have also chosen important settings to reinforce their message. In 2003, when George W. Bush announced the end of the War in Iraq, he did it on a giant aircraft carrier.

men and several horses into two dugout canoes and a 55-foot (18-meter) long boat. The party traveled into the wilderness, and Jefferson waited eagerly for their return.

In autumn 1806, Jefferson received exciting news. Lewis and Clark were back in St. Louis. In three years, the expedition had traveled thousands of miles and filled notebooks with observations. They described bears that stood as tall as men and rivers thick with enormous salmon. They wrote of the rugged Rocky Mountains and the misty beaches of the Pacific Ocean. They described the American Indian tribes that lived and hunted on the vast, grassy plains.

Jefferson was not the only president who used the office to support science and exploration. John Quincy Adams, an educated and refined man, believed the young republic would achieve greatness through better schooling. He said that knowledge was the greatest tool to improve life. Adams called on Congress to build schools, research centers, and observatories for scientists to study the heavens. "Light-houses of the sky," he called them.

Another president, John F. Kennedy, was not satisfied with just observing objects in space. He pushed Americans to find a way to travel to the moon.

Into Space

In the 1950s, the two most powerful countries on Earth, the United States and the Soviet Union, sought to control space. The Soviet Union took the lead in 1957 when the country

launched a small satellite called Sputnik into space. Americans were horrified as Sputnik orbited Earth, crossing high over the United States.

The Americans responded by building their own rockets. By the early 1960s, both nations had successfully sent people into space and returned them to Earth. Both nations planned to be the first to land a man on the moon. John F. Kennedy, the new president, wanted that person to be an American.

At a meeting with space experts, he asked how much it would cost. About $40 billion, the experts thought, which was a huge sum at that time. The experts warned that it would probably take ten years and that the Soviets may get there first anyway.

The United States was able to get a man on the moon in large part to the efforts and encouragement of President Kennedy.

Kennedy was not satisfied. "I want some answers," he snapped. "Ask the janitor over there if you have to. But I want to know how and when we can get to the moon."

It would take nine years, billions of dollars, and the work of more than 400,000 people. On July 20, 1969, a small space capsule landed on the moon surface on an area called the Sea of Tranquility. An American astronaut clambered out of the spacecraft and set his foot into the gray powder on the surface.

"That's one small step for man," said astronaut Neil Armstrong, "one giant leap for mankind."

Into the Future

The presidency has changed enormously since George Washington. In this period of more than two hundred years, the presidency has grown into the most powerful and recognized leadership position in the world. Wherever a traveler goes in the world today, from a crowded city in Brazil to an isolated fishing village in Japan, almost everyone can name the president of the United States.

One thing, however, has not changed about the presidency. They have all been white men. Except for John F. Kennedy, who was Catholic, all have been raised Protestant.

The presidency is always changing, however, and this appears to be changing as well. More African Americans, especially a general named Colin Powell, were recently considered serious candidates for the presidency. Several potential female candidates in both the Democratic and Republican parties made strong showings in the polls.

We can't predict the next president, but we can be assured that the presidency itself will survive. When George Washington first became president, there was a king in France, a czar in Russia, and an emperor in China. None of those leadership positions exists in those countries today, but the presidency still endures.

To Mars?

Space has not lost its grip on the American imagination. In 2004, President George W. Bush announced that more money should be set aside for a manned mission to the planet Mars. While many were worried about the program's cost, others were thrilled by the idea of further space exploration.

Timeline

1787	Delegates in Philadelphia write the office of the president for the Constitution.
1789	George Washington is sworn in at Federal Hall, New York City, to become the nation's first president.
1794	Settlers in Western Pennsylvania rebel against a whiskey tax in July. George Washington leads the army to crush the rebellion.
1800	John Adams becomes the first president to sleep in the newly constructed White House in Washington, D.C.
1804–1806	Ordered by President Thomas Jefferson, an American expedition led by Lewis and Clark travels across the western part of the North American continent and back again.
1829	Andrew Jackson's inauguration leaves the White House in tatters when a crowd of his supporters follow him into the executive mansion.
1830	President Andrew Jackson issues the first of many vetoes.
1835	A man tries to shoot Jackson on January 30. He fails and is confined to an asylum.
1860	Abraham Lincoln is elected president in November. South Carolina secedes in December, and the nation is on the verge of civil war.
1861	The Civil War begins. President Lincoln uses the powers of the presidency to save the Union.
1865	Lincoln is shot by John Wilkes Booth in Ford's Theater on April 14. He dies the next morning.

1868	President Andrew Johnson is the first president to be impeached. He is not, however, removed from office.
1881	President James Garfield is shot by a furious office seeker on July 2. He dies more than two months later.
1901	President William McKinley dies on September 14 after being shot twice in the abdomen on September 6.
1905	President Theodore Roosevelt brings together Japanese and Russian negotiators to end their war. He wins the Nobel Peace Prize for the effort.
1917	President Woodrow Wilson asks for a declaration of war against Germany in April. The United States enters World War I.
1919	President Wilson takes a tour to promote his peace plan and the League of Nations to the American people in September. The peace plan is later voted down, and the United States does not join the league.
1929	Herbert Hoover is inaugurated president during a period of general prosperity. On October 24, however, the stock market crashes, and the country enters a period of terrible economic depression.
1933	Franklin D. Roosevelt is sworn in as president. He promises the nation a "New Deal" to restore economic growth on March 4.
1935	The Social Security Act, an important element of the New Deal, is passed on August 14.
1940	Roosevelt runs for, and wins, the presidency for a third term, an unprecedented feat.
1951	The Twenty-Second Amendment, which prevents any president from holding more than two terms, is ratified. President Truman relieves General Douglas MacArthur from his command of UN troops in South Korea.

Continued on next page

Year	Event
1963	President John F. Kennedy is assassinated in Dallas, Texas, on November 22.
1964	A North Vietnamese ship allegedly fires torpedoes at American ships in the Gulf of Tonkin. President Johnson uses this incident to send American troops to South Vietnam.
1969	American astronauts land on the moon on July 20.
1974	Because of the Watergate scandal, Richard Nixon resigns from the presidency on August 9.
1978	President Jimmy Carter brings together Israeli and Egyptian negotiators, who resolve their bitter differences and declare peace.
1981	A gunman shoots President Ronald Reagan on March 30. He survives the attack.
1998	President Bill Clinton admits having lied about a relationship with a former intern, Monica Lewinsky. Clinton is later impeached by Congress but is not removed from office.

Glossary

asylum—a prison or hospital for mentally-ill patients

blockade—the act of blocking a nation from trade with the outside world

checks and balances—the powers the three branches of the federal government use to block each other and prevent one branch from gaining too much power

civilian—a person who is not a member of the armed forces

Congress—a governmental body made up of representatives voted into power by their fellow citizens. The U.S. Congress has two bodies: the Senate and the House of Representatives.

Constitutional Convention—the group that met in the summer of 1787 to reform the Articles of Confederation. The convention drafted the Constitution. It has also been called the Federal Convention or the Philadelphia Convention.

depression—a severe economic downturn that causes business failures and job losses

federal government—the government that has oversees the entire country, as opposed to state, city, or local governments

pardon—the act of excusing people for their crimes

precedent—an action done for the first time that establishes how people or institutions will act in the future

secede—when a group leaves an organization to form their own

term—the amount of time an elected politician serves before facing an election

veto—the president's act of rejecting a law passed by Congress

To Find Out More

Books

Beschloss, Michael, ed. *American Heritage Illustrated History of the Presidents.* New York: Crown Publishers, 2000.

Boller Jr., Paul F. *Presidential Anecdotes.* New York: Oxford University Press, 1997.

Davis, Kenneth C. *Don't Know Much About the Presidents.* New York: HarperCollins Juvenile Books, 2001.

DeGregorio, William A. *The Complete Book of U.S. Presidents.* New York: Random House, 1997.

McPherson, James M., ed. *To the Best of My Ability: The American Presidents.* New York: Dorling Kindersley, 2001.

Rubel, David. *Scholastic Encyclopedia of the Presidents and Their Times.* New York: Scholastic Trade, 2001.

St. George, Judith. *So You Want to Be President?* New York: Philomel Books, 2000.

Videos

American Experience: The Presidents Collection. PBS Home Video, 1994.

American Presidents: The Most Powerful Men on Earth. BFS Entertainment and Multimedia, 1998.

Presidents in Crisis: Johnson Quits and Nixon Resigns. A & E Home Video, 1999.

Upstairs at the White House: Private Lives of U.S. Presidents. A & E Home Video, 1999.

Organizations and Online Sites

American Presidents: Life Portraits
http://www.americanpresidents.org
This website, created by C-SPAN, contains biographies of the presidents and interactive videos of presidential moments. The site also has a tour of presidential grave sites.

Federal Hall
http://www.nps.gov/feha
Federal Hall was the spot where George Washington was first inaugurated in and where the first federal Congress met.

Grolier Online Presents the Presidents
http://ap.grolier.com
Grolier Online has assembled its extensive articles on presidents and the presidency on this website. The site includes a gallery of presidents and information written for various grade levels.

Independence National Historic Park
http://www.nps.gov/inde/index.htm
This national historic park is the site of the birth of the United States government.

Monticello
http://www.monticello.org
Thomas Jefferson's home in central Virginia includes information on Jefferson's life and career.

The White House
http://www.whitehouse.gov/history/presidents
The White House maintains a Web site that offers biographies of each president as well as information on life in the White House.

A Note on Sources

For general sources on the presidency, I consulted two excellent books: *To the Best of My Ability*, edited by James McPherson; and *American Heritage Illustrated History of the Presidents*, edited by Michael Beschloss. Both volumes were filled with details and good introductory essays on the office. For individual studies of presidents, I read James Flexner's *George Washington: The Indispensable Man*; Edmund Morris's *The Rise of Theodore Roosevelt*; Stephen Oates' *With Malice Toward None: The Life of Abraham Lincoln*; Doris Kearns Goodwin's *No Ordinary Time: Franklin and Eleanor Roosevelt*. Another great book on the presidency is Kenneth Walsh's *Air Force One: A History of the Presidents and their Planes*, which gives a number of anecdotes describing how presidents acted in personal settings.

—Brendan January

Index

Numbers in *italics* indicate illustrations.

Adams, John, 39–40
Adams, John Quincy, *38*, 49
Armstrong, Neil, 51
Assassinations, 40–43

Begin, Menachem, 30, *31*
"Black Thursday," 18
Booth, John Wilkes, 40–41, *41*
Branches of government, 9, 11
Bush, George H. W., 37
Bush, George W., *12*, 48, 51

Cabinet, 18
Carter, Jimmy, 30–31, *31*, 48
Checks and balances, 11
Civilian Conservation Corps (CCC), 20, *21*
Clark, William, 47, 49
Cleveland, Frances, 16
Cleveland, Grover, 16, 40
Clinton, Bill, 23, 45
Clinton, Hillary Rodham, 16
Confederate States of America, 24–25
Congress, 9, 11, 25–26, 29, 30, 45, *45*, 49
Constitution, 9, *10*, 29
Constitutional Convention, 9
Coolidge, Calvin, 34–36, *35*
Czolgosz, Leon, 42

Dean, John, 43
Democratic National Committee, 43

Executive branch, 9

Federal Bureau of Investigation (FBI), 43, 44
Federal Hall, 8
"Fireside chats," 20–21
First ladies, 16
Ford, Gerald R., 44
Ford's Theater, 41, *41*

Garfield, James, 41
Grant, Ulysses S., 36–37
Great Depression, 18, *19*
Guiteau, Charles, 41
Gulf of Tonkin, 29

Hoover, Herbert, 17–19, *17*, 37
"Hoovervilles," 18, *19*

Impeachment, 45, *45*
Inaugurations, 20, *20*

Jackson, Andrew, *14*, 15–17, 40, *45*
Jefferson, Thomas, 36, 39, 46, 47, 49
Johnson, Andrew, 45
Johnson, Lyndon, 13, 29, *29*, 40
Judicial branch, 9

Kennedy, Caroline, 36
Kennedy, Edward, 44
Kennedy, John F., *36*, 37, 40, 42, *42*, *48*, 49, 50, 51
Kennedy, John, Jr., *36*
Korean War, 27

Lawrence, Richard, 40
Laws, 15
League of Nations, 25, 26
Legislative branch, 9
Lewinsky, Monica, 45
Lewis, Meriwether, 47, 49
Lincoln, Abraham, 24–25, 41, *41*, 45
Livingston, Robert, 8

MacArthur, Douglas, 27–28, *28*
McKinley, William, 42
Military, 13, 15, 16, *22*, 23, 24, 29
Moon landing, 50–51, *50*
Mount Vernon plantation, 8

Nixon, Richard, 43–45, *44*, 48, *48*
Nobel Peace Prize, 30, 31

Oswald, Lee Harvey, 42

Pan-American Exposition, 42
Pardons, 11, 44, 45
Powell, Colin, 51
Presidential oath, 8, 13
Public Works Administration, 20

Randolph, John, 16
Reagan, Nancy, 16
Reagan, Ronald, 16, 43
Reconstruction, 45
Resignation, 44, *44*
Revolutionary War, 7
Roosevelt, Alice, 34
Roosevelt, Eleanor, 16
Roosevelt, Franklin Delano, *12*, 19–21, *20*
Roosevelt, Theodore, 30, *32*, 33–34

Sadat, Anwar, 30, *31*
Salary, 34
Social Security Act, 20
Soviet Union, 27, 49–50
Sputnik satellite, 50
State of the Union address, 27
Supreme Court, 43

Taft, William Howard, 37
Tennessee Valley Authority, 20
Term limits, 21
Thanksgiving, 45
Tonkin Gulf Resolution, 29
Truman, Harry S., 27–28, *28*, 40
Twenty-Second Amendment, 21

Veto power, 11
Vietnam War, 29–30

War, 11, *12*, 13, 23
War Powers Act, 29, 30
Washington, George, *6*, 7–9, 13, 18, 24, 39
Watergate, 43–45
Watergate Office Complex, 43
Whiskey Tax Rebellion, 24, *24*
White House, 16, 33, 34
Wilson, Edith, 16
Wilson, Woodrow, 16, 25, *26*
World War II, *12*
Writ of Habeas Corpus, 25

About the Author

Brendan January is an award-winning writer of more than twenty-five books for young readers. A graduate of Haverford College and Columbia Graduate School of Journalism, January has written for the *Philadelphia Inquirer* and *The Record.* He is a Fulbright Scholar and currently lives in northern New Jersey with his wife and daughter.